Conflict Resolving Communication

A Skill Development Approach

Conflict Resolving Communication
A Skill Development Approach

William Daniel Semlak
Illinois State University

Waveland Press, Inc.
Prospect Heights, Illinois

For information about this publication, write or call:

Waveland Press, Inc.
P.O. Box 400
Prospect Heights, Illinois 60070
(312) 634-0081

Printed in the United States of America.

KM
7-6-83

Contents

Preface

Developing communication skills useful in a wide variety of situations is an important objective of education. Conflict situations occur often in everyday life. In both our interpersonal relations with others and our more formal relationships in our work environments we constantly find ourselves in conflict situations. *The purpose of this book is to provide insight into what communication skills are useful in dealing with conflict.* The book is divided into four chapters to achieve this goal. Chapter One discusses the inevitability of conflict in our culture while Chapter Two presents communication concepts especially useful to understanding conflict resolution. Chapter Three focuses on the skills used to help resolve a conflict in which an individual is directly involved, while Chapter Four focuses on the skills necessary to help others resolve their conflict.

Conflict Resolving Communication: A Skill Development Approach should be an especially useful book in several situations. It would be especially appropriate as a textbook in a Conflict Resolution course or as a supplementary book for a course in Interpersonal Communication, Small Group Communication or Argumentation. Perhaps the book's greatest value would come as a supplementary textbook in a Management course.

The material presented in the book forms the basis for a number of management communication training programs developed by the author. The book is an excellent resource for management training programs because it includes considerable skill development advice and is short enough that it can be used in a time-compressed educational environment.

1

Conflict in Society

One central characteristic of American institutions constant throughout national development is plurality. Americans are proud that within the political, economic, religious, social, and moral spheres they have allowed and often mandated a diverse set of institutions. This phenomenon—often asserted as the distinguishing characteristic of American culture—forms a basis for conflict in our culture. Conflict appears to be an indispensable element of American culture which offers both an essential guarantee of freedom and at the same time threatens much of our societal order. This chapter will first discuss the institutionalization of conflict in the political, economic, religious, social, and moral spheres of life.

Culturally Ingrained Causes of Conflict

Political

We need look no further than the constitution to see seeds of diversity and potential conflict in American society. The founding fathers had little confidence in government so they devised a system of checks and balances to insure that many forces would be competing for control and power in government. We are all aware of the conflict between the power of the president and the power of the Congress, the power of the federal government and the power of the states, the power of the Senate and the power of the House of Representatives.

The entire political decision-making process in the United States has been described as a "free marketplace of ideas."

This viewpoint reinforces the importance of conflict in our political process. In the "free marketplace of ideas" it is assumed all political positions compete in open discussion and debate. All viewpoints are subject to critical examination by both supporters and critics. Within the process conflict between opposing factions is essential because the system assumes those positions which can stand the test of debate in the "free marketplace of ideas" are those which should emerge and be adopted by society as a whole.

As a result of checks and balances and the assumption that political ideas should be tested in the "free marketplace of ideas," considerable political conflict may be observed. For example, President Johnson committed a large number of troops to Vietnam. While in the early stages few openly questioned this policy, as the war grew and United States' objectives appeared unattainable vigorous conflict manifested itself in several forms. While some chose the channels of debate and discussion to express their dissatisfaction with the Vietnam policy, others chose channels of confrontation, dissent and violence. Yet the entire process reflected the operation of conflict within the American political process.

More recently political conflict has emerged over our energy policy. President Carter advanced an energy policy that focused attention on energy companies and their role in society. Much of his proposal was never passed because in the "free marketplace of ideas" his proposal could not win out over the interests of the oil companies. It would be easy to conclude that much of our legislation is the result of powerful forces resolving conflict over issues.

Legal

The legal system offers an additional example of the institutionalization of conflict in American government. When someone feels he has been wronged, often he takes legal action. Within the adversary system of the judicial process individuals find an institutionalized channel for resolving most civil conflict.

Within recent years there has been a proliferation of quasi-legal institutions designed to resolve conflict. Many states have instituted small claims courts in which a small claims referee attempts to resolve minor civil issues short of a formal legal process. Such procedures usually require citizens to attempt to resolve their problems through communication. Other extensions of our legal system include formal hearings designed to resolve conflict. If someone charges that unfair labor practices exist, it is typical to have a formal hearing at which both sides present their cases and an official agency recommends a solution.

Economic

Our American "mixed market" economy has evolved from a free enterprise system much as Adam Smith described in *The Wealth of Nations*. A central assumption of such an economic system is competition. Theorists contend that free competition between various producers promotes the best use of economic resources. Inherent in this competitive framework is conflict. Throughout the market system conflict can be observed as an integral part of the system's operation.

Current labor-management negotiations provide an example of economic conflict. Because resources are scarce both management and labor wish to maximize their share of the profit from production. Labor and management attempt to settle their differences through a variety of communication strategies. Sometimes representatives of labor and management can arrive at an agreement through informal discussion of the issues. However, it is not always that simple. From time to time a variety of more sophisticated bargaining strategies have to be employed by both sides. Often an impasse leads to a strike or lockout. Perhaps professional negotiators or arbitrators are brought in to aid in the conflict. In major strikes, the president might invoke the Taft-Hartley Act to force a cooling-off period. During the entire process a variety of communication factors come into play.

The growth of regulatory agencies and departments exacerbates the occurrence of conflict within the economic realm. The Atomic Energy Commission (AEC) provides an example of a growing adversary relationship between economic interests and society as a whole. When a firm wishes to build a nuclear power plant, for example, a variety of conflicts may emerge. Groups may oppose the site of the proposed project and the power company must solve the conflict to get a construction permit. As the project progresses, the AEC may question the safety of the operation and the company must resolve any conflict between itself and the AEC before construction can continue. Once the plant is in operation, the AEC continuously monitors the operation. A wide variety of discretionary actions that the AEC may choose to take could generate conflict between the company and the AEC.

As economic institutions become more complex, more and more examples of agencies designed to regulate and control aspects of the economic system will emerge. The inherent conflict between factions in the economic system is certain to further institutionalize conflict in economics.

Religious

One form of diversity well institutionalized in American society is a tolerance for religious difference. Since many of the early settlers migrated to the American colonies in search of religious freedom, it is not surprising that such freedom was established within the Bill of Rights and in state constitutions. While the various religious elements seem to leave each other alone in regular church matters the implication of religious plurality in terms of public conflict is awesome.

Within recent years the political front has witnessed a growing area of concern. In *The Real Majority*, Scammon and Wattenberg observed that a shift from the economic issues which dominated the "New Deal" political era occurred around 1968. In place of the "Economic Issue" a collection of issues referred to as the "Social Issue" emerged as central to American politics. Among other things the "Social Issue" includes such questions as abortion, legalization of drugs, civil rights, rights of women, and senior citizens. The "Social Issues" differ from the "Economic Issues" in that their resolution involves addressing deep-seated moral issues. Very often the factions separate along religious lines. For example one of the strongest anti-abortion groups in the United States is the Catholic Church.

The importance of understanding conflict along religious lines is exacerbated by some of the implications for resolving conflict based on religious belief. As I will suggest later in the book often conflict is resolved through a mutual compromise among all parties involved in the conflict. In such a situation each party gives up something while working toward a solution. However, when dealing with religious beliefs one often deals with attitudes central to an individual's belief system. More important, the attitudes are primary and sacred to the individual. Thus the resolution of conflict based on religious values often cannot be accomplished through the more traditional bargaining processes because the various factions will not engage in give and take.

During the 1980 elections a new religious force called the "moral majority" appeared supporting candidates who articulated positions consistent with their beliefs. Many have suggested that the success of the moral majority and candidates whom they backed in 1980 signals an increased focus on the resolution of societal issues based on religious and moral beliefs.

Thus, while religious plurality may facilitate personal freedom, students of conflict resolution must recognize that it may hinder solving much of our social conflict. Inherent within the multiplicity of religious belief systems are diverse noncompromising positions.

Conflict Prevention and Resolution

It is often said that "the only things that are certain are death and taxes." While many would be tempted to add other items to this list, any comprehensive list of potentially certain things would be incomplete without conflict. Conflict appears to be an inevitable condition of our daily existence. Husbands quarrel with wives, teachers disagree with students, neighbors argue with each other, fellow employees bicker with each other or their supervisor. The list of routine conflict in our society goes on and on.

The purpose of this book is to help you understand conflict, the causes of conflict, and how you can use communication as a tool to deal with conflict in your everyday life.

A common misconception in our understanding of conflict is that in some way conflict is an abnormal condition. This view suggests that people who have conflicts are failures because they allowed conflict conditions to exist. People who subscribe to this viewpoint often feel guilty when they disagree with others and they often avoid issues, individuals, or situations because they feel that an uncomfortable conflict situation may arise.

A more realistic view of the nature of conflict views conflict as a healthy part of human relationships. Whether considering close interpersonal relationships or a large organizational setting, it is inevitable that individuals will have incompatible goals, needs, wants, or desires. This condition is likely to spawn conflict. To suppress incompatible goals, needs, wants or desires, merely to avoid conflict could have a profound long-term effect on either the relationship or the organization and would likely only result in future conflict.

For individuals to maximize their ability to deal with conflict, it is recommended that they view their roles in relation to conflict from the viewpoint of both *conflict prevention* and *conflict resolution.*

Conflict prevention involves developing a set of skills that enable an individual to recognize conditions that are likely to spawn conflict, identify the elements that are contributing to the potential conflict situation and then prevent a serious conflict through intervention in the process. For example, a sales manager at a large corporation may observe two of the sales team starting to fight over rights to a new client. The manager might recognize that both members of the sales team played some role in getting the new client. Rather than allowing the two salespersons to fight over the "rights to the new client," the manager calls both of the salespersons into his office and indicates that they will share the new client and split the commission. The conflict was avoided by the manager having a clear perception of a likely area of competing desire among his salesworkers, and his intervention prevented a conflict from developing.

Conflict prevention skills are useful in both large organizational settings and close personal relationships. The husband who can anticipate sources of conflicting needs between himself and his wife can then intervene in an inevitable clash between his needs and his wife's needs, and avoid serious marital problems. For example, the husband may need to get away from the pressures of his job and desires to take a leisurely vacation at the beach. The wife, on the other hand, may need to get away from the rather routine home duties and desires to take a very active vacation trip to the city to visit all the stores, museums, and attend all the cultural events. He perceives a trip to the city as just more pressure like he has at work and she perceives going to the beach as just as routine as home duties. A potential conflict can be avoided if the husband recognizes his wife's needs and suggests a vacation plan that involves both some time at the beach and some time in the city. For this intervention to be successful, it is necessary for the husband to communicate not only his suggested vacation plan to his wife, but also to communicate his needs and desires and to show how his proposed solution is designed to satisfy both of their needs and desires.

Conflict resolution involves the solving of a conflict once it exists. A conflict resolution situation is said to be a *mixed motive* condition. A mixed motive situation is one in which the involved parties have both a motive to cooperate and a motive to compete. The motive to compete suggests that individuals involved in a conflict recognize that their goals differ from the goals of the other parties in the conflict, while the motive to cooperate suggests that both parties want to resolve the conflict and recognize that they will have to work together to achieve that end. Three levels of conflict resolution will be discussed in this book as samples of mixed motive conflict resolution situations: *negotiation* or *bargaining, mediation,* and *arbitration.*

Negotiation or *bargaining* refers to a face-to-face interaction between the conflicting parties. In such a situation, each side recognizes that the conflict is a "no win—no lose" situation in which each side must compromise. However, it is possible that despite both sides approaching the conflict in such a manner, no solution can be worked out. In such a situation, mediation may be the next step. *Mediation* refers to bringing in a third party to help the conflicting parties resolve their conflict. A mediator uses skills in communication and persuasion to assist the conflicting parties to resolve their conflict. At times a mediator is unable to bring conflicting parties together. In these situations, arbitration is often used. *Arbitration* refers to bringing in a third party to hear the facts of the case and then to make a decision binding on the conflicting parties.

All three of the above conflict resolution situations reflect the assumption that both parties involved in the conflict have both the motive to compete and the motive to cooperate. The major difference is the type of *communication interaction* used to achieve resolution of the conflict. In bargaining, *cooperative discussion* is employed while in mediation *cooperative discussion is arranged through a third party.* In arbitration the interaction takes the form of presentations of material to a third party. *Very different communication skills are necessary to be effective in the three different situations.*

2

Communication in Conflict

Americans have responded to conflict in society with the belief that communication is a critical tool for resolving conflict. During the post-revolutionary period, for example, Americans developed a sense of pride and respect for the idea that the "American way" of resolving political conflict utilized discussion and debate of the issues rather than the use of force. Historians point to the role of the Henry-Madison debates over ratification of the Constitution, the Webster-Clay debates over slavery and the Lincoln-Douglas Senate campaign debates as examples of the American commitment to rational discussion of conflict and resolution of such conflict through communication.

Unfortunately, such a view does not provide the complete answer for conflict resolution. The Civil War is only one example of historical inability to use communication to resolve conflict. Today is the age of the "Communication Breakdown." At every level of human interaction communication breakdowns exacerbate conflict. The Arabs cannot communicate with the Israelis, the Irish Catholics cannot communicate with the Irish Protestants, the old cannot communicate with the young. Parents and children, brothers and sisters, teachers and students, faculty and administrators, all are purported to experience communication breakdowns from time to time. Communication, which to many represents the solution to conflict, in such an age becomes a barrier to conflict resolution. Today, many problems escape resolution because people cannot communicate.

Communication and Conflict Resolution

Classical rhetorical theory contributes much to our understanding of the role of communication in the conflict resolution process. In his *Rhetoric* Aristotle outlined the role of public speaking in classical Greek life. Two types of public speaking noted by Aristotle involved conflict resolution. The first — often called *forensic* speaking — involved speaking in the courts. When conflicts over such things as property rights arose, Greek citizens were called on to present their cases to the courts. The courts would listen to the arguments presented by all the parties in the dispute and then would make a decision based on the strength of the case.

A second role of public speaking related to conflict resolution outlined by Aristotle has been labeled *deliberative* speaking. Greek political issues were settled by open citizen participation in a democratic form of decision making. Conflict over issues of public policy were settled by citizen debate over the merit of the issues with the eventual policy being selected by voting. Although forensic and deliberative speaking are usually studied under the topic of persuasion, it is important to consider them under a study of conflict resolution. For example, it is clear that early Greek tradition established a principle of conflict resolution being a rational process. Both forensic and deliberative speaking emphasize the use of rational argument and logic as tools in resolving conflict. It is also clear that the early Greeks viewed the resolution of conflict as an adversary relationship.

The focus provided the dominant contribution of communication tradition to conflict resolution throughout most of the present century. The belief was that knowledge of logic and good reasoning and the ability to communicate one's positions in a logical, well-supported manner would provide each individual with the tools necessary to resolve conflict.

During the 1940's and 1950's the communication tradition started to consider resolving conflict from a discussion perspective. The discussion perspective suggested that groups of individuals discovered the answers to problems that created conflict through the systematic group investigation of a problem. Using a systematic method of inquiry, often the reflective thinking process of John Dewey, individuals would objectively sit down and discuss common problems and come to a solution acceptable to all parties through consensus. Although the deliberative and forensics traditions mentioned above stressed individuals resolving conflict by convincing others of the correctness of their position, the discussion tradition emphasized individuals resolving problems through give-and-take and the discovery of solutions acceptable to all parties in the conflict.

More recently, during the 1960's, a third tradition in the field has contributed to our understanding of conflict resolution. Concern about communication and its impact on the relationship between the parties in communication was discussed by many authors. Watzlowick, Beavin and Jackson (1967) argued that any communication included two elements: content and relationship. This means that in communication "what is said," "how something is said," or "what something that is said actually means" is very much influenced by the relationship between the participants in the communication. The importance of this tradition to conflict resolution rests in the growth of concern for interpersonal climate in conflict resolution. Such variables as trust, willingness to communicate, and communication style were found to be important in the development of conflict resolution effectiveness. For example, in some conflict situations a low level of trust among the parties involved in the conflict results in a very slow disclosing of information. The communication climate in such a conflict is very different from the climate found in relationship building communications discussed elsewhere in this book.

Later in this chapter we will see how the three traditions mentioned above are central to our understanding to the three levels of conflict resolution discussed in this book. Much of our knowledge about bargaining and negotiation comes from research in interpersonal communication, discussion and group communication. In addition, what we know about mediation is very much influenced by research in group decision-making, especially in the area of consensus. Arbitration, on the other hand, draws heavily from the classical tradition of deliberative and forensic speaking.

Experience demonstrates that for anyone to become an effective agent of conflict resolution, he or she must develop the proper attitude toward resolving conflict. Historically three personal factors seem essential to resolving conflict. To become an effective conflict resolution agent, one must recognize these personal factors. First, the persons must be willing to work hard to overcome conflict. Very often conflict is not resolved because the involved individuals fail to try hard enough to overcome communication breakdowns. How many times have you failed to patch up a disagreement with someone because you were unwilling to communicate with the other person? Conflict will not solve itself. Individuals must view themselves as active communicating agents when they are involved in conflict and take active roles in trying to overcome conflict by overcoming the communication breakdown fostering it. Conflict resolution requires *active communication.*

A special responsibility for conflict resolution rests on the shoulders of those trained in communication. As you finish your study of communication you should realize that you have gained special insight into the problems of communication. In your everyday interactions you will encounter people who do not understand how their communication contributes to the conflicts in which they are involved. As you deal with these people you should assume the role of a conflict resolution clinician. You should develop the ability to apply your skills in communication to conflict situations in ways that will help those lacking communication skills resolve their conflict. Later in life you might find yourself in a civic group attempting to deal with a government agency. A conflict over the future location of a highway may have generated considerable conflict. Your skills as a negotiator may be critical to resolution of the conflict. At the same time you may have to teach each member of your bargaining team about communication so that they may effectively contribute to the deliberation without jeopardizing the negotiations. Perhaps you may find yourself in a management position in which you have to teach your employees to develop a communication style that will help them avoid constant bickering. In such a situation you may find yourself having to apply your communication skills to situations which involve conflict between people who do not understand why their communication causes problems for them. In such a role you will have to act as a communication clinician teaching your workers how to communicate with each other. Your skill in communication will become a valuable commodity which you must share with others to resolve conflict.

A second personal factor essential to your becoming an effective conflict resolution agent is a recognition that you may need to modify your personal communicative behavior to be effective. People have a tendency to blame the other parties in conflict for all the communication breakdowns that occur. How many times have you felt that your problem could be solved if only the other person would listen, or not be so irrational, or would compromise. Most people tend to view their own behavior as acceptable and try to blame the other party's failure to adapt for their own failure to communicate. Everyone has to realize that before someone can become part of the solution, he must recognize that he is part of the problem. Conflict resolution demands that each individual reexamine his communication and determine what it contributes to the conflict. Once the individual makes that determination he must be willing to modify his communication. He must be willing to admit that his past communicative behavior may have been a cause of the problem and must adjust his communication accordingly. This is very difficult. Communication is a very important part of self-image. Often it is very difficult for an individual to recognize that something that he or she does when he or she communicates contributes to conflict and communication breakdown. Yet everyone must make this adaptation to effectively resolve conflict. Conflict resolution requires *adaptive communication*.

A third personal factor essential to becoming an effective conflict resolution agent is the recognition that *conflict resolution is a delicate social science which can be learned*. For the past several years scholars in communication, psychology, political science, economics, and related fields have attempted to formulate the scientific study of conflict resolution. These scholars have approached conflict resolution from a variety of perspectives and conducted numerous experiments to determine the principles that reduce conflict. The years of study have demonstrated that conflict resolution is a multidimensional, extremely complex process. We have observed that certain principles seem useful in resolving conflict and that in general the most useful way to overcome conflict is a systematic application of principles to the problem. This book as well as others in the field reports much of the systematic base of conflict resolution. To become an effective conflict resolution agent you must recognize that effective conflict resolution requires *systematic efforts to solve the problem.*

The systematic concept becomes especially important when considering arbitration. For arbitration to be successful the parties involved have to establish procedures as well as systematic argument to maximize their position. The Toulmin Model of argument will be suggested as a specific method of systematic argument.

Types of Conflict

Various authors have examined conflict from numerous perspectives. Conflict has been examined throughout a wide range of social processes. *Intrapersonal conflict* refers to the conflict that an individual faces when he is forced to make choices. A variety of human motivation theories have been advanced in an attempt to understand how man resolves intrapersonal conflict. One common theory suggests man attempts to resolve intrapersonal conflict by making choices in such a way as to maintain a state of internal balance. This theory contends that man works toward a level of internal consistency in his intrapersonal conflict resolution. While examination of theories of intrapersonal conflict resolution is interesting, for the most part it is outside the scope of this book.

Interpersonal conflict involves the behavior betweeen two or more persons working toward a goal that either is mutually exclusive or is not completely attainable by all parties. Interpersonal conflict is most often studied within the framework of a dyad. A considerable amount of research has been completed utilizing a variety of two-person games to gain an understanding of how individuals perceive conflict and react in dyadic situations.

The dyad is not the only situation in which interpersonal conflict is found, however. Triads contain some unique interpersonal conflict situations. Unlike a dyad a triad offers the opportunity for two members to gang up on the third by forming a coalition. The communication strategies employed in triad conflict resolution must recognize a variety of coalition formation problems and their implications.

Often interpersonal conflict is found among a larger number of people. One general principle of conflict behavior suggests that the larger the number of factions involved in a conflict the greater the number of options and the greater the number of unrealistic positions. Also as the number of people involved in interpersonal conflict increases, communication flexibility decreases. The range of positions acceptable to all parties decreases as the number of participants increases. Interpersonal conflict represents a complex phenomenon that offers a wide variety of communication options.

Conflict may also be examined within a group context. *Intragroup conflict* refers to conflict among members of a group. Understanding intergroup conflict is predicated both on understanding the nature of the particular group under consideration and on the group's relationship to other groups and to society. Groups develop in society to serve different purposes and function in different ways. An understanding of group dynamics is essential in overcoming many types of intragroup conflict.

Intergroup conflict occurs when groups in society work toward ends which are mutually exclusive or not completely attainable by all groups simultaneously. An increasingly complex society experiences a growth in pressure groups such as the American Medical Association, the National Rifle Association, Common Cause and other special interest organizations. Very often these groups compete with each other for scarce resources or with government agencies in an attempt to shape public policy.

Communication Variables Important to Conflict Resolution

Communication Style and Conflict

Individuals seeking to improve their communication in conflict situations often find the recognition of diverse communication styles a useful tool. Not only does each person engage in a pattern of communication that reflects a certain style but the various individuals with whom one comes into conflict may have very different communication styles. As one becomes experienced in conflict resolution one realizes that certain styles are highly compatible and individuals using them find conflict resolution easy while other styles are often somewhat incompatible and individuals using them have difficulty solving their problems.

Although many different characteristics make up a total communication style, two elements are important when considering an individual's conflict resolution style. Individuals differ in their *assertiveness* and *cooperativeness* levels. By assertiveness we mean the willingness of an individual to emphasize the satisfying of his/her own needs while recognizing the rights and needs of others while communicating. An individual is said to be *nonassertive* in conflict situations if he or she adopts a passive communication style that does not communicate his or her needs or feelings to the other parties in the conflict. Nonassertive individuals often are shy and passive and face problems by hoping that they correct themselves. The non-assertive individual has little self-confidence and often finds it difficult to gain the respect of others. An *assertive* individual, on the other hand, is able to handle conflict by the skillful expression of his or her personal needs, wants, and desires but without attacking others or dictating a solution. Assertive individuals usually are confident and have the respect of others.

Cooperativeness, on the other hand, reflects the extent to which an individual attempts to satisfy the concerns of the other parties in the conflict. Uncooperative individuals often adopt *aggressive* postures by either overtly or covertly working to hurt, humiliate or threaten the other individual. Aggressive persons are highly insensitive to the feelings and needs of other participants in the conflict. Their actions usually provoke resentment in others.

Assertiveness and cooperativeness combine to form five different communication styles (Kilmann and Thomas, 1975). Each style contains different attitudes toward conflict and as a result different responses in a conflict situation. Figure 1 represents the five communication styles identified by Kilmann and Thomas.

Figure 1

Summary of Kilmann and Thomas' Communication Styles

Style	Characteristics
Competing Style	High Assertive Low Cooperation
Accommodating Style	Low Assertive High Cooperation
Avoiding Style	Low Assertive Low Cooperation
Collaborating Style	High Assertive High Cooperation
Compromising Style	Moderate Assertive Moderate Cooperation

A *competing* style is often employed by a person who is assertive but uncooperative. Such a person pursues his or her own objectives at the expense of others. A competing individual employs power-oriented strategies to achieve an objective. Such strategies include the ability to argue, the use of status and position, or the use of threats. Individuals who tend to compete generally perceive that they are standing up for their rights, defending what is right, or trying to win.

An individual who is unassertive and cooperative is said to be employing an *accommodating* style. The accommodating style is the opposite of a competing style in that an individual neglects his or her own concerns in an attempt to meet the concerns of the other individuals in the conflict. A person who chooses to use an accommodating style tends to avoid conflict situations when possible but once he or she becomes involved accommodating manifests itself in self-sacrifice, obeying orders he or she would prefer to disobey, or yielding to a point of view he or she does not hold.

The *avoiding* style includes unassertive and uncooperative characteristics. The avoiding individual does not immediately pursue either his or her concerns or the concerns of others. Rather, he or she does not address the conflict, often pretending it is not there. An avoider might sidestep the controversy, attempt to postpone treatment of the issue, or actually withdraw from the situation.

Opposite of the avoiding style is the *collaborating* style, which includes both assertive and cooperative elements. A collaborating individual attempts to work with others until a solution is discovered that fully satisfies the needs of all concerned parties. For a collaborating style to be effective the individuals in the conflict have to identify their underlying concerns and explore alternatives that are compatible. Collaboration requires a willingness of the individuals in the conflict to disclose considerable information and a high level of trust between the conflicting parties. Collaboration may include analysis of the disagreement to learn from each other's insights and trying to find creative solutions which eliminate the basic source of the problem.

A *compromising* style includes a mix of assertiveness and cooperativeness. Compromising individuals attempt to find practical, expedient, mutually acceptable solutions. The compromising style includes elements of the four styles above. A compromising individual gives up more than a competing individual but less than an accommodating person. In addition a compromiser addresses issues more directly than an avoider but not in as much depth as a collaborator. Many would argue that the compromising style is the best communication style in a conflict resolution situation because an individual maximizes his or her ability to find the solution best for all parties involved in the conflict.

However, as Murdock and Semlak (1980) point out each of these five styles can be appropriate and functional. A key factor necessary to deal with conflict is *flexibility*. Each communication style is appropriate in some instances, but inappropriate in other instances. For example, suppose your spouse wants to discuss buying a new car but you are tired and have a headache. An effective strategy in this case might be avoidance. That is, when an individual is under stress the forced discussion of a topic tends to produce conflict. However, the use of an avoidance strategy can only work in the short run because the issues will eventually have to be dealt with to avoid frustration and resentment. Eventually you will have to select one of the four remaining communication styles. You may give in to your spouse and buy a sports car (accommodate) because you believe the issue is not important. On the other hand, you may argue strongly for a van (compete), if you feel strongly about the issue. You may compromise and suggest buying a station wagon as opposed to either the sports car or the van. Or you may collaborate and agree to buy a used sports car and a used van rather than spending the same amount of money on a new car. *The most important point to remember related to the five possible communication styles is that you should develop the ability to use whichever style is most appropriate in a given situation.*

As indicated earlier in this chapter to be an effective conflict resolution agent it is necessary to be active, adoptive and systematic. Thomas and Pondy (1979) suggest that an individual achieves this end by adopting a set of communication strategies designed to maximize the management of conflict. They suggest such an inventory of communication skills would include *scanning, explaining, preparing, excusing,* and *repairing* communication.

Scanning involves soliciting feedback from others. Statements such as "What do you think?" or "Do you have any problems with this?" are examples of scanning communication. Scanning is useful because it encourages the other party in a conflict to provide you with information. You increase your ability to select the appropriate communication style if you have more information about the other person's feelings, wants, and desires.

Explaining includes statements such as "What I really meant was..." or "I don't think that you really understand what I am trying to say." The purpose of explaining is to minimize conflict caused by misunderstanding. Solving conflicts based upon real differences is hard enough without having additional fuel added to a conflict because a misunderstanding occurs.

Preparing statements are used to give advanced warning of upcoming statements or behavior that may be perceived in a negative way. Such statements as "I regret to inform you that..." or "Due to circumstances beyond my control..." are examples of preparing statements. The effective use of preparing statements enables an individual to minimize the negative effect of transmitting certain material. This hopefully will enhance the source's ability to reduce conflict.

Excusing statements involve comments designed to convince someone that messages which may be perceived in a negative manner were not malicious or arbitrary. There are three types of excusing statements. *Unintentional excusing* statements consist of such statements as "It was an accident" or "I was not aware of the fact." These statements suggest that the source should be excused because the behavior or communication was unintentional. *No alternatives excusing* statements attempt to excuse behavior or communication on the ground that the individual was "forced" to take the action. Comments such as "I had no choices," "I could not help it," or "It was forced on me by others" are examples of no alternatives excusing statements. *Legitimate excusing* statements suggest that even though an action or communication was perceived in a negative way, that should be excused because it was justified. Statements such as "you deserved it" or "our procedures required it" are examples of legitimate excusing statements.

Repairing statements are designed to make up for past errors and in general improve the relationship between the conflicting parties. *Apologies* such as, "I'm sorry," "It was my fault," "I was in error" are repairing statements, while *penance* statements are repairing statements that attempt to make amends. "Please let me do this for you," "What can I do" or "Let me help you with this" are examples of penance statements.

Anyone wishing to become effective at preventing or resolving conflict should become familiar with the strategic use of the above communication skills.

3

Bargaining and Negotiation

Using Interpersonal Communication Skills

Bargaining or negotiation is an informal form of conflict resolution. Developing effective bargaining skills is largely a matter of using good interpersonal communication techniques in dealing with a conflict. Often the communicative behavior of the parties involved in conflict attempts to resolve the situation through achievement of a mutually acceptable arrangement. This strategy involves an attempt to achieve consensus or negotiate a position acceptable to all parties involved. Inherent within such a strategy is an assumption that all parties will approach the conflict willing to bargain. In other words, each party approaches the bargaining table with the recognition that they will have to give up part of their original demand in order to achieve a settlement. At the same time they recognize that the other party will be in the same position and that the final outcome will be somewhere between the two initial positions. Such a situation should produce an atmosphere in which risk to parties is minimized because the outcome produces no absolute winners or losers. For example, in labor relations management and labor both approach the bargaining table with a series of positions. Each recognizes it is unlikely that the final outcome will represent either of the initial positions. Rather, both sides recognize the final outcome will reflect a position that will emerge during mutual give and take. This type of communicative behavior falls into the broad category of bargaining.

One of the most important points to recognize here is that bargaining is a rather informal method of conflict resolution. On a day-to-day level each one of us is constantly bargaining to resolve conflict. You want to buy a stereo from your friend. He wants $100.00 but you do not think it's worth that much. You point out to him that the system is seven years old, that the components are tube rather than solid state, that it is not compatible with most new equipment. You then offer him $75.00.

You get a test back. It is graded "D". You feel that the grade is not indicative of your understanding of the subject matter. You go in to see the instructor. He says he is sorry that you did not do better on the test but there is nothing that he can do for you. That is your cue to start bargaining. You suggest that perhaps you could do extra work? Perhaps you could take the test over? Perhaps you could count the next test double? You pose as many alternatives as you can and hope to work out a better grade. Your strategy is designed to make the instructor feel that he is being unreasonable if he does not accept one of your options. Here you appear to be reasonable—willing to accept any option. Your strategy will hopefully encourage him to bend and accept one of the options.

Bargaining in such situations is largely a matter of interpersonal communication strategy. You put yourself on the line. You initiate the communication, you suggest the options, you take the risk, you force the other party to act. You shift guilt to the other party if bargaining breaks down. More important you often attempt to appeal to personal prestige and honor to achieve a settlement. You promise to do better on the next test, to come to class more often in the future, to study harder, all to impress your opponent with your bargaining sincerity.

The above example represents only one of the simplest examples of bargaining in a dyad. Only two factions are represented and one member has very little at stake. The outcome will largely be dependent on the student's shifting a sense of guilt to the instructor and encouraging him to adopt a more flexible policy. On occasions the number of factions involved in the bargaining process increases. At times the interpersonal dynamics of the interchange are not so simple. While a number of factors contribute to the communicative effectiveness of the participants in bargaining the following considerations seem especially important:

Individual communication flexibility is effected by the number of parties involved. In general, whether dealing

with intragroup or intergroup conflict, the greater the
number of factions involved the more difficult it is to
find a position acceptable to all parties. As the number
of parties in a conflict increases two important things
happen. First, the chances increase that even the most
unrealistic positions will receive significant support.
This hinders later attempts to compromise without
various factions losing face. Second, often an elaborate
set of coalitions emerge which complicates later communication. During the coalition formation process
various factions of the conflict verbalize and commit
themselves to positions which they later find difficult to
maintain. The Middle East provides an example of this
principle. While we often tend to oversimplify the conflict there as the Arabs against the Israelis, this simply
is not the case. The Arab faction includes a variety of
countries from Egypt to Syria to Saudi Arabia. The factions include a variety of ideologies, the PLO (Palestine
Liberation Organization) to groups willing to coexist
with Israel as things are today. Importantly the variety
of Arab factions has fragmented the Arab position and
allowed almost every viewpoint to have a voice in the
deliberations. The Middle East is a prime example of
reduced communication due to the number of factions
involved.

*Public commitment to positions hampers bargaining
effectiveness.* A very important condition necessary to
effective bargaining is keeping options open. The participants must avoid placing themselves in positions
which will be difficult to change. For example, once a
party in a labor negotiation publicly states his union
"cannot accept any settlement without an 8% raise,"
he may find it impossible to compromise at 7%. Individuals involved in bargaining should not only avoid
making any public commitment which would tie them to
a position but they should also avoid any communication which might force the opposition to make a public
commitment. Several years ago a teachers' strike was
averted only by a stroke of luck after an irresponsible

commitment was made by the school board chairman. During a television interview he inadvertently compared his teaching salary scale to that of a nearby town and said that there was "no way" a settlement greater than 6% was justified. The teachers saw it differently and were holding out for an 8.8% settlement. Considerable public support was behind the teachers but the board chairman stuck to his position. Despite erosion of support from other board members the chairman became identified with the 6% figure and felt that he could not give in to the pressure. Finally, just before the strike was to occur a board member found a loop-hole for the board chairman. It appeared that the nearby town that the chairman had compared his teachers to had a much superior fringe benefit package. The board member explained to the chairman that he could grant the 8.8% settlement but still not exceed the other town's total salary and fringe benefit scale. While the logic of the argument may not have been compelling, it provided the board chairman just the excuse he needed to accept the 8.8% level and still save face.

Status of the participants is an important consideration in bargaining. In general when all members involved in the bargaining are of equal status all members have to adopt a communicative strategy that involves the presentation of nonrigid positions. However, when some participants in bargaining have significantly higher status than others they often bargain from more rigid positions. This strategy's inherent risk is that the low status participants may perceive the bargaining position as too rigid. They may respond by withdrawing from the exchange or by developing rigid positions of their own. Parents often rely on status to resolve family conflicts. They simply tell you that you will stay home on Saturday and cut the grass and like it. While the short run benefit of getting the grass cut is probably facilitated by reliance on status and authority, the long run impact of such behavior on the relationship is uncertain.

The more fixed the size of the "pie" the greater the propensity of conflict. As we indicated in chapter one the economic factor of scarcity contributes to much of the conflict in American society. During a period of growth, for example, public universities with few exceptions experienced increases in enrollment and financing. Each year the "pie" available increased and most universities received more. In such a situation University X's increase was not at the expense of University Y's increase. Communication within such a framework tends to be self-oriented. Each university outlines its particular needs and gains a larger share of the growing pie. However, in the 1970's when college enrollment started to stabilize we witnessed intense competition for the more fixed pie of higher education. During the 1980's this competition should increase even more leading to greater potential conflict.

Group Communication Principles Related to Negotiation

While the above considerations discussed the importance of several factors on bargaining effectiveness separate consideration of some additional factors related to group conflict merits consideration. As we indicated in the second chapter, conflict may occur either within or between groups. Some important considerations related to intragroup conflict include:

Numerous factors influence the motivation of members within a group to solve conflict between members. Although this concept involves a variety of factors which interact to affect individual members' motivation levels, most principles of group conformity seem important to group members' willingness to bargain in intragroup conflict. If a member likes the other members of a group, there seems to be a greater propensity for him to initiate bargaining. Thus individuals highly committed to a group are much more likely to bargain to reduce intragroup conflict than those with a lower level of commitment. At the same time several factors appear to influence a member's bargaining position within a group. The degree to which a member of a group respects the opinions of the other faction is very important to that member's willingness to modify his initial positions during bargaining. If a member of a certain faction has established high credibility in the past in terms of supporting positions valuable to the group's overall objectives, this credibility often serves as a powerful incentive for members of opposing factions to modify their positions. In addition, if a person who has high credibility within the group also has high status in the group this further increases the likelihood that the lower status, lower credibility members of opposing factions will bargain in an open and honest manner with the high status, high credibility member.

Some factors, however, have a negative impact on a group member's willingness to enter into intragroup bargaining. Group members are less likely to enter into bargaining with other intragroup factions on issues which they perceive as unimportant to the group as a whole, or on issues which they perceive as tangential to the group purpose or identity, but very important to themselves.

Intergroup conflict is often necessary for intragroup cohesion. Many people ignore the fact that a group may seek conflict with external agencies to promote unity. As a member of a group it is important to understand that intragroup conflict can often be resolved by generating intergroup conflict. Group members who appear firmly committed to positions, and rigid in bargaining, often drastically modify positions to achieve the unity necessary to defeat an external opponent. Political parties are notorious examples of such behavior. Prior to candidate selection, various factions compete intensely. However, as the general election nears and the opponent from the opposing party appears, compromise and consensus are often achieved within the party to present a united front.

Intragroup conflict is often resolved through establishment of group norms. Sometimes a group may choose to bypass normal processes of conflict resolution by establishing group norms which minimize the possibility of conflict. For example, a fraternity during its initiation procedure attempts to eliminate prospective members who do not sufficiently acclimate themselves to the group culture. In doing this the fraternity minimizes many possible sources of future intragroup conflict by establishing norms which minimize the sources of conflict.

Communication Strategies

When engaged in bargaining certain types of strategic communications may be important. As we indicated in the last chapter a systematic approach to conflict resolution is useful in maximizing the effectiveness of one's efforts. The following communication strategies seem to have potential to improve one's bargaining ability.

Sincere Communication

The most essential preliminary communicative behavior that a bargainer should master is sincere presentation. Sincere communication involves two dimensions: bargaining in "good faith" and an impression of bargaining in "good faith." A bargainer must bargain in good faith to be viable. This requires absolute willingness to fulfill all terms of the solution. An intermediary must always avoid bargaining beyond his authorization.

As important as bargaining in good faith is the perception in the minds of the other parties that the bargain is in good faith. A negotiator who has a record of overextending his bargaining authority is of little value because the parties in the negotiations may perceive him as nontrustworthy. Certain ritual behaviors are useful in giving the impression that bargaining is in good faith. Early in the negotiations a bargainer may take extreme positions from which he can back down quickly and move toward middle positions. He may take breaks to consult with other members of the negotiating team or with the principals he represents. One stylistic characteristic of a bargainer who is establishing a perception of bargaining in good faith is the use of tentative language. Try to avoid talking in absolutes when "probably" and "possibly" may be used. Then only after the position is firmed up should you take a definite position. The appearance of good faith negotiation is essential for a bargaining agent.

Nonpolarizing Communication

As mentioned earlier in this chapter the bargaining situation is one in which the parties involved reach a settlement in which each maximizes his position within a framework of a solution acceptable to all parties. Polarization communication is an impediment to such a goal. Polarization communication is communication which portrays the issue at hand in a win-lose situation. Such communication portrays the various positions as miles apart and suggests that any settlement will be at the expense of one party's central issues. Much of the current controversy in Ireland is exacerbated by the polarizing nature of the communication. Both involved parties talk in terms of any settlement requiring complete control of policies for their side. Such communication exacerbates bargaining tension. When such tension exists parties do not enter into open bargaining. They perceive the risk as too high and often engage in what we will classify later as avoidance communication. When polarization communication takes place early in the bargaining process it is essential that a new bargaining agent be found or that the present agent be encouraged to modify his rhetoric. If the polarization is caused by factors other than the bargaining agent it is essential to reduce bargaining tension by reassuring the other party that no position the other side perceives as a loss is essential to the settlement. Polarization communication violates the principles of limited risk and mutually acceptable solutions essential to the negotiation process.

Signposting Communication

To avoid high risk induced bargaining tension, custom dictates bargaining signposts. Bargaining signposts are communications which establish the parameters in which a negotiation can take place. Early in the negotiations each faction should establish signposts which identify high risk bargaining tension areas. For example, one non-negotiable demand of a student radical group may be amnesty for the participants in a demonstration. The group may have held a demonstration primarily to draw attention to their position and feel that at present they may negotiate any of the initial issues which led to the demonstration. However, they may believe their future success in involving nonmembers in demonstrations rests on gaining amnesty for demonstrators. During negotiations in such a situation the bargainers would signpost such a position by threatening to leave the bargaining table and resume demonstrations every time the administrators question the amnesty issue. The administrators would soon realize the student faction perceived refusal to grant amnesty in a win/loss perspective. The students would signpost this area as a high risk bargain tension raising issue. The administrators are not required to give in to the amnesty demand, but they are warned of a source of high risk bargaining tension by the students' effective signpost communication.

Flexible Communication

An effective bargainer develops a flexible communication strategy before entering the negotiation. First, "musts" will be established. He/she will determine the minimum compromise his/her side can accept. Then the bargaining issues which are the least important will be determined. These become "give" points. Flexible bargaining requires a careful weighing of "give" points. At the same time the bargainer will learn as much about the opponents' position as possible. During the negotiation a bargainer will have to trade "give" points with the opposition. He/she must be careful not to give too easily to the opponents. At the same time bargainers have to know what their "musts" are and gain as many "musts" as they can. American foreign policy negotiations often display considerable art in trading "give" points. While negotiating a settlement to the war in Vietnam the release of the American prisoners of war was a "must" for the American delegation. Since the representatives of the Republic of North Vietnam recognized this fact they were able to trade almost all our "give" points for that "must" point. On the domestic level, divorce settlement often involves such "must" points as possession of the house, car or children, and such "give" points as paying for the child's education, paying the life insurance premium or taking possession of the pet goldfish.

An effective bargainer also maintains a flexible bargaining style. The communication approach should vary to fit the presentation. At times the bargainer must demonstrate a firm temperament. At times a conciliatory approach is best. Some circumstances demand a hostile approach to shake the opponent or to get a vital message across.

Avoidance Communication

Resolving conflict requires that all parties involved recognize that conflict exists, and communication must take place to resolve it. On occasion parties involved in conflict choose to retreat from communication by avoiding the issue. Sometimes parties in the conflict refuse to confront the other parties but instead complain about the conflict to others. Often in businesses, workers complain about their working conditions to their fellow workers. For one reason or another they did not get the raise that they deserved. The problem becomes so serious as far as they are concerned that their work is affected. Yet these same individuals when confronted by their superior say that everything is all right. This situation illustrates how status may become a deterrent to open communication. Rather than discussing the issue the party avoids communication on the topic.

Such a condition aggravates the conflict and hinders the resolution of the problem. A closely related situation involves the party who encourages conflict by telling others about his dissatisfaction but denies that a problem exists when confronted by the factions involved. Sometimes individuals within businesses use such strategies to jockey for position within the power structure. Conflict within such a context has little possibility of being resolved. Avoidance communication precludes the solving of conflict because both parties do not accept the underlying assumption of bargaining that a mutual solution can be achieved.

Often when an attempt to resolve conflict is in progress another type of avoidance communicative behavior appears — a party in the conflict attempts to change the subject. Sometimes when the conversation reaches the most sensitive part of the conflict one or more parties try to shift the focus to another subject. Effective bargaining requires overcoming all forms of avoidance communication. Individuals have to force others to come to grips with the sensitive area of discussion.

Misdirected Communication

Another kind of communication which hinders effective bargaining is misdirected communication. This involves a variety of strategies which attempt to focus attention off the point of conflict and on to other issues. One type of misdirected communication attempts to make the other parties in the conflict feel guilty for their role in the conflict. This is a typical situation observed in interpersonal conflict. Often a lover's quarrel over an issue boils down to one side trying to get the other party to admit the problem was all their fault and take the entire initiative in making up. While this can be an effective strategy *if* one party accepts the entire blame for the situation it will more likely exacerbate the conflict.

This type of communication is also often observed in situations involving individuals with role differences. Parents often try to convince their children that the problem is all their fault. Such situations often do include successful examples of making one party in the conflict assume the entire blame but often the outcome is the other party taking even more rigid positions.

A much better approach would have the parties involved in the bargaining attribute blame for the problem to inevitable circumstances, some unnamed third party, mutual misunderstanding, or something of this nature. The "guiltless crisis" is easier for both parties to solve. When neither party is blamed for the conflict neither has to respond in a defensive way.

An additional example of misdirected communication is communication which focuses on aspects of the opponents' lives irrelevant to the conflict at hand. Perhaps two years ago the parties had a conflict over another matter. References to such a conflict only increase bargaining tension and do nothing to improve the current situation. Often misdirected communication involves random attacks on the past life of the parties involved in bargaining. Such a communication strategy only increases the rigidness of the attacked parties' positions and does little to promote bargaining.

Sometimes misdirected communication takes the form of a trap. One party in the bargaining process may say, "Let's be totally honest with each other." After the other parties in the bargaining process lay their cards on the table not only does the trapper refuse to lay out his position but he attacks the other position as totally unacceptable. Avoiding the trap situation is especially critical during bargaining. Information should always be revealed gradually and positions modified incrementally.

Misdirected communication often takes the form of character analysis during the bargaining process. After someone expresses a feeling or opinion such misdirected communication will attempt to tell everyone how the person "really feels" by interpreting what was said in a different way. Inherent in character analysis is an attempt to undermine the credibility of a bargaining opponent by casting doubt on his sincerity, credibility, motivation, or on some other factor.

Interpersonal Skills

When bargaining, not everyone approaches the bargaining table with the same interpersonal skills. Certain personal behavior inhibits bargaining. The participants must have a sense of the appropriate communication at all times during bargaining. For example, a sense of humor and wit are useful tools in reducing bargaining tension. However, they must be employed at the correct moment. Just as a bargaining opponent is making a serious point a joke is not in order. Bargaining should include the perceptive use of humor.

A person engaging in bargaining also needs to refrain from over-personalizing himself in the bargaining process. Often there is a tendency to perceive the opponent's attack on positions as a personal attack. Individuals who are too ego-involved with positions make poor bargaining agents since they interpret attacks against positions as attacks against themselves. They become defensive and emotional. Rather than evaluating the substance of the opponent's position they respond with rigid, aggressive, defensive arguments. The effective bargainer has the ability to remove himself from personal involvement with the issues.

The good bargainer also develops critical listening skills. Listening in a bargaining situation requires remembering what has been said and utilizing that information effectively. When appropriate, a good bargainer takes notes. In formal bargaining situations both sides often tape record bargaining sessions and study the verbal interaction. Several parties form a bargaining team; members often pool their mental notes after each session to maximize their picture of what occurred.

Numerous suggestions are advanced to aid listening effectiveness. Such common advice as listening for main ideas, concentrating on the subject at hand, compensating for issues to which you react emotionally, maintaining a relaxed physical position, taking breaks to avoid overload, all contribute to an effective personal listening style.

Bargaining agents must also learn to recognize the meaning of nonverbal cues during discussion. Facial expressions, body tension, hand movements, eye contact, posture, vocalic features, all potentially communicate important information. An effective bargainer must be able to determine when he has gained all he can on an issue; when he is on a sensitive issue; when his ideas are perceived as acceptable. Interpreting nonverbal communication may be the most important factor in making such assessments. The effective bargainer must also learn how to control nonverbal cues. Generally the best bargaining style will sort out as many unintentional nonverbal cues as possible. The bargainer hopes to eliminate all misleading cues and cues which give away feelings he would prefer to hide. Effective bargainers, much like poker players, attempt to minimize giving away their hand through nonverbal cues.

In general, personal communication skills such as tact, common sense, and courtesy contribute to the effectiveness of bargaining. However, attempts to be overly cooperative or friendly often are interpreted by others in bargaining as rhetorical ploys. One should always recognize that bargaining is essentially a confrontation situation in which both parties, through give and take, attempt to resolve a conflict. Parties in conflict quickly recognize the reality of the situation and are not victimized by overly submissive role portrayals.

Negotiation is a highly complex communication encounter. While we often negotiate in a largely informal setting, negotiation also includes some highly formal communication. As you can see from this chapter your ability to bargain is determined by a wide variety of communication skills.

4

Mediation and Arbitration
Using Interpersonal and Public Communication Skills

The previous chapter discussed the dynamics of conflict resolution within the context of mutual interdependence. However, at times individuals involved in conflict are unable to resolve their misunderstanding within this context. Often, for example, professional athletes are unable to negotiate contract arrangements. Despite considerable efforts for one reason or another, the parties involved cannot reach a common solution. One or more parties in the conflict may believe they have reached their minimum acceptable positions. One party involved may be reluctant to continue bargaining because he believes the other party is not bargaining in good faith. Regardless of the reason, a bargaining impasse precludes settlement.

Often such a conflict is resolved through third party conflict resolution. This chapter will explore the dynamics of third party conflict resolution. This should not be confused with employing a bargaining agent. Often within formal bargaining such as collective bargaining sessions, the principals are represented by trained bargainers. This does not represent third party conflict resolution. Third party conflict resolution includes either *mediation* or *arbitration*. In *mediation* a third party is called in to facilitate the bargaining process. For example, during the recent hostage crisis, many countries and individuals attempted to mediate the conflict between the United States and Iran. Finally, the crisis was solved through an Algerian delegation which functioned as a catalyst in resolving the problem. A small claims court referee often functions in the same fashion. The referee's duty is to mediate disagreements by convincing the parties involved to compromise toward a common settlement.

Often squabbles between children are mediated by the parents. The department chairman in a university might find it necessary to mediate a conflict between factions of the faculty. The boss at work mediates an argument over who will take their vacation during June. Throughout society within a wide range of situations, various individuals are required to mediate conflict. In all of these instances, the mediator tries to facilitate the resolution of conflict by bringing the parties together. The role of the mediator is essentially that of a persuader.

Arbitration, on the other hand, involves granting the power to a third party to study the conflict and to reach a solution which is binding on all involved parties. Civil matters are usually resolved in this fashion. If two businesses are in conflict over a contract, for example, they will probably attempt to resolve the conflict by trying to negotiate a mutually acceptable solution. If that fails, they may call in a third party to act as a mediator, to advise them. If that fails, they may take the issue to court. In court, all the facts would be presented and the judge or jury would render a decision binding all parties to a solution.

Both mediation and arbitration are forms of third party conflict resolution. Both are more formal than negotiation and involve considerable ritual. Communication skill is important to both forms of conflict resolution and different strategies are involved in each.

The above definition provides a useful distinction between mediation and arbitration. It is very important to note that both procedures are described in the pure form. In society a variety of forms have emerged which often are called arbitration or mediation but do not fit these definitions. Labor disputes are often solved by nonbinding arbitration. In such a situation, both parties present their position to a third party. The third party then examines the data and presents a solution. Unlike in regular arbitration, either party may reject the solution. In some instances the arbitrator has different powers. Normally the arbitrator may decide on any solution that he/she believes equitable. Professional baseball has established arbitration procedures under which the third party has no power to adjust the solution. The arbitrator listens to the facts and then decides which side has the stronger case and that position is binding on both parties. This procedure is designed to deter arbitration and encourage mediation or negotiation because it is in both parties' best interest to try to achieve a decision. By going to arbitration, they risk more than by giving up a bit more in negotiation.

In society, mediation and arbitration operate in many forms. While the material presented in this chapter will focus primarily on the pure forms, the concepts have considerable application to all forms. In addition, much of the material will also be useful for negotiations because many of the interpersonal strategies may be used in that setting.

Mediation

Individuals constantly find themselves in positions in which they have to assist other parties in resolving conflict. Two friends who are bickering should be brought together, your brother and sister who are fighting should be reconciled—just to mention two common examples of conflict which require mediation. Mediation is an important skill in business and professional life. Increasingly large corporations and industries experience internal conflict. Any management level position requires mediation abilities to bring competing factions together. The following communication variables are important to mediation.

An Effective Mediator Has High Credibility

Credibility is usually defined as the perceived image of a person in terms of trustworthiness and expertise. That is, someone who is said to have high credibility is perceived as both knowledgeable and reliable. These are both essential characteristics for mediation. For example, a fraternity president might be called upon to settle a dispute between the pledge chairperson and the treasurer.

An Effective Mediator is Neutral

Often you will find your friends involved in disputes. Your ability to mediate the conflict will be predicated on your being perceived as neutral. To be an acceptable mediator, you should refuse to become ego involved with either position. You should not make any statements which could be interpreted as taking a position on the issue. If either party has any reason to believe that your sympathy lies with the other party, your ability to mediate will be reduced. Marriage conflicts often demonstrate this point. Often troubled parties confide in their friends and seek advice. Sometimes a well-meaning but inept friend tries to bring the two parties together by mediating the conflict. Unless the friend carefully maintains an absolute aura of neutrality — very difficult since a friend is usually closer to one marriage partner than to the other — his or her efforts are usually worthless or even harmful. All kinds of behavior may contribute to this failure. Even minor things which happened several years ago may cast doubt on his or her neutrality. This suggests a reason why trained marriage counselors are effective. Not only are they well schooled in common marriage problems, but they can easily establish themselves as neutral third parties. Often a zero history mediator — one with no previous relationship with either party — has the best chance to be perceived as neutral.

An Effective Mediator Manages Contact Between Parties

Mediators are often called in because the parties involved are unable to achieve anything constructive through face-to-face communication. The parties may be hostile toward each other and personal contact may increase the hostility. A mediator must be able to sense when face-to-face contact is desirable and when it should be avoided. Sometimes it is useful to call a meeting between the involved parties early in the mediation process. At such a meeting, each side should be instructed to present their positions. Such a meeting is useful for the mediator to assess the level of disagreement and the actual positions. The meeting also gives the mediator useful indications of the amount of future contact between factions that he or she should arrange. The mediator may observe that the parties involved are receptive to listening to the other side and determine that contact will facilitate understanding. On the other hand, the mediator may conclude the significant private sessions are necessary before the factions can gain anything through face-to-face communication. Often lawyers working on out-of-court settlements never bring the parties together when mediating a settlement because the hostility between factions is so intense, progress would actually be retarded.

Flexibility is the key to party contact management in mediation. No rigid formula offers the answer. Often preliminary interviews with the factions give sufficient insight to determine the amount of contact desirable. On other occasions, only actual contact gives the mediator the insight necessary to gauge the amount of future contact which will facilitate resolution of the conflict.

An Effective Mediator Manages Rumor

Those who mediate conflict, especially in large institutional settings, recognize that one of the biggest barriers to conflict resolution is rumor. Rumor may be generated and transmitted by both parties involved in the conflict and by parties not involved at all. An effective mediator always develops channels to monitor rumor so that he or she is aware of it. He or she will try to find noninvolved parties in key locations who will inform him or her of any rumors which may be operating against resolutions of the conflict. An alert mediator will also develop communication strategies to counter rumor. He or she will flood the system with counterevidence when necessary to disprove rumor; he or she will consult with the parties involved to dispel rumor; he or she will discredit the rumor source to stop rumor. Often the presence of rumor will require the mediator to bring the parties together to dispel it. Actual face-to-face presentation of issues sometimes is the only effective tool a mediator has to counter rumor. Such a situation sometimes can have a highly positive effect on the mediation. If considerable tension between sides was built up by rumor, the effect of breaking down the rumor often operates as a threshold which encourages future mediation. A very skilled mediator can use rumor to his or her advantage but the risk is high. If rumor cannot be dispelled, it often exacerbates the conflict.

An Effective Mediator Knows When to Listen

Usually a mediator is brought into a conflict that is well developed. Before the mediator can be effective, he must understand every aspect of the conflict. He or she will encourage all parties to tell him or her the whole story in private sessions. Often minor facts which neither party mentions are important to the conflict. To be effective, the mediator must discover these facts. In listening, the mediator often functions as a tension reliever. Often talking to the mediator gives the parties in the conflict a chance to ventilate their hostilities. Once such hostilities are out in the open, the mediator can help each party overcome feelings which must be modified to resolve the conflict. Such an internal tension reducing process may be the prime agent of conflict resolution.

The mediator also listens to get the facts straight. He or she sorts out those things on which both sides can agree. He listens for any hint of common ground. He or she tries to determine what rumors have contributed to the conflict. He or she tries to determine what are the maximum acceptable positions of both parties. He or she determines who are the leaders of both factions who might possibly be most susceptible to changing their opinion, and who might work as opinion leaders for him later in the process. In short, the mediator listens for anything and everything essential to solve the conflict.

An Effective Mediator Conveys Information

Often while meeting separately with the parties, the mediator will discover information which should be conveyed to the other side. An effective mediator, however, is very strategic about what information he or she conveys and the manner in which it is presented. In a hostile situation, a mediator will often temper the remarks conveyed so that the intent of the message remains intact but the emotional connotations are removed. Information which one side wants conveyed to the other side but the mediator feels could inhibit the conflict resolution process is often suppressed. A skilled mediator conveys information very selectively. He or she will carefully evaluate everything and pick key phrases, ideas, and concepts and present them to the other side. Items which could form the basis of a breakthrough on an important issue are highlighted in the presentation of information. Overstatement is avoided at all costs and material is presented tentatively rather than absolutely. The mediator tries to convey material in a way which maintains communication flexibility and position flexibility for both sides.

An Effective Mediator Promotes Internal Inquiry

Mediation requires considerable effort to get parties in conflict to modify their positions. An effective mediator will encourage the parties to reevaluate their positions constantly. He or she will encourage the participants to try to separate complex issues and consider them in smaller units. He or she will probe their positions with them, searching for points of potential compromise. Often the mediator plays devil's advocate presenting various alternatives, some of which are obviously unreasonable, in an attempt to place an issue in perspective or show the number of options availble. The mediator in this respect functions as a resource person offering the parties in the conflict information and ideas to promote inquiry.

An Effective Mediator Uses Allies

Within any faction, many perspectives exist. Often the mediator identifies members of the factions inclined to adopt middle ground positions and encourages them to rally the support of the other members. Sometimes the allies are not members of the faction but interested bystanders who can easily influence the members. Recently a university committee mediating a dispute between warring departments encouraged the president of the university to send each department a letter encouraging them to accept the compromise worked out by the committee. Upon receiving the letter, each department somewhat reluctantly moved toward the compromise position. This demonstrates the extent to which some mediating agencies go to gain ally support for their settlement. One co-ed who was trying to mediate a lovers' quarrel convinced the boy's roommate to pressure his buddy to apologize in return for a date.

Within the factions in conflict, certain parties are more prone to change than others. In addition, some parties serve as opinion leaders within the faction and wield a powerful influence over the rest of the members. Often mediators approach such members and sell them on helping solve the problem. Such a strategy requires the mediator to shift from his or her mediator role and approach the individual on the interpersonal level. Often mediators use their personal prestige to convince such members to serve as their agents. Often they suggest rewards to the individuals such as "you can take credit for the idea" to enlist their support. Business managers often find the best way to mediate conflict within an organization is to decide themselves how to resolve the conflict and, to insure that the conflicting parties accept the compromise, heap lavish praise on the parties involved for their efficient settlement of the conflict. The surprised parties quickly support the compromise which they received acclaim for establishing. Mediators often find the use of interpersonal influences essential to success. Statements such as "I've worked hard for months, and I'm afraid it will have been for nothing unless you can help me out;" "If you could just see yourself clear to accept this, I'll buy the beers;" or "If you could do me one small favor" are all approaches to using interpersonal influences in medition.

An Effective Mediator Minimizes Risk

Conflict resolution involves bringing parties together in such a way that various factions give up something that they want in the settlement process. Within this process, there is inherent risk that a side will perceive it is losing too much. Effective mediators attempt to convince the parties involved that they can shift their positions without losing face. In addition, the mediator attempts to convince each party that they are not losing significant ground and reminds the parties of the ground the other factions are giving up.

Mediation then may be described as the "art of persuasion."

We advanced the above hints as general strategies to employ in mediation. Be sure to remember that most of the concepts designed to help you bargain more effectively are also useful in mediation. It is also important to recognize that mediation involves a more risky conflict resolution situation for the participants. In negotiation, it is often quite possible to develop a solution that is perceived as acceptable by all parties involved. However, in mediation, the risk to the involved parties is increased because it is more likely that a solution acceptable to the other parties in the conflict will require an individual "giving up" important points. Thus, an effective mediator needs to convince the involved parties to modify their positions. This may be achieved by showing how the other side is giving up points to be reasonable; by telling a faction that they can gain strategic advantage by giving up a position; by asking a party in the conflict to look at his/her own position because you think it might need to be modified. In short, a good mediator is often forced to. persuade the conflicting parties to move closer so that the final solution does not seem to be one in which only they are giving up important issues.

Arbitration

So far, this chapter has examined face-to-face bargaining during which the conflicting parties have been able to resolve their differences, and mediation through which third parties have been able to assist conflicting individuals or groups to resolve their conflict. Often conflict situations reach a point where neither bargaining nor mediation are capable of resolving the differences and in such a case, often arbitration results. Arbitration involves both parties in the conflict situation presenting their positions to a third party who decides which side has the best case and then selects a decision that is binding on all parties. For example, in a university, it is possible that both the History and the Philosophy departments want to offer a course entitled "History of Philosophy." University policy might preclude two departments offering the same course, so the departments attempt to resolve their conflict. First the chairpersons meet and try to solve the problem through bargaining, but they are unsuccessful. Next, the chairperson of the college curriculum committee might attempt to mediate between the two departments but, again, the conflict remains unresolved. Finally, both parties take their case to the Dean, who has the power to arbitrate the situation and to make a decision binding on both parties. The Dean, for example, might decide the History department will offer the course; he may decide that both departments will cross-list the course and teach it alternate semesters; or he might decide neither department should offer the course until new faculty resources become available to teach it.

Situations such as the one above happen in everyday life more than you might think. Parents arbitrate conflicts between children, fraternity officers arbitrate conflicts between members, and small claims referees arbitrate conflicts between citizens. More and more, positions of management require skill at both presenting cases during conflict and resolving conflict based on the cases presented by conflicting parties. In the courtroom, juries and judges listen to both sides of cases and then make decisions, thus arbitrating such conflicts as civil suits and divorce settlements.

The central thrust of this treatment of arbitration will be on the development of the skills necessary to make one's case and present it to an arbitrator. Parties in arbitration situations soon learn that they have a burden of proof. The burden of proof is essentially the responsibility of each party to assemble the arguments and evidence necessary to convince the arbitrator that their position is correct.

When you have a conflict with another party and you wish to settle it through arbitration, you operate much like a lawyer in a trial or a college debater. You assemble all the facts and arguments that you can marshal together and attempt to convince a third party arbitrator of the wisdom of your position. You will employ evidence in such a way as to construct arguments which you believe cannot be countered by the opposition. To accomplish this, you need an understanding of proper argument, reasoning and evidence.

Argument is usually referred to as the inferring of conclusions from data. Perhaps the most useful way of looking at argument is the Toulmin Model of Argument. The Toulmin model of argument includes six parts which combine to form a complete argument. The model is divided into two parts: the essential and the secondary. The three essential parts of the model exist in any argument. Even the simplest argument you and a friend present when you ask another friend to decide if you should go to the movies or the ball game requires three components. The three essential parts of the Toulmin model of argument are: data, warrant, and claim.

> *Data* is the evidence you use in the argument. It includes the facts, opinions, statistics, examples, and testimony that are employed.

> *Warrant* is the mental leap which enables you to infer the claim from the data.

> *Claim* is the position you are supporting. It is the conclusion that you want the third party to reach.

The following hypothetical example should clarify the essential parts of the Toulmin argument. Suppose ballplayer Tom Smith is presenting his case to an arbitrator. He may be arguing that he deserves a 25% pay increase. When he presents his case, he points out to the arbitrator that last season he played in 25 percent more games, hit 25 percent more home runs, stole 25 percent more bases, and made 25 percent fewer errors. He then argues that since he improved his contribution to the team by 25 percent, he ought to get a 25 percent pay increase. The argument would be diagrammed on the Toulmin model as follows:

Figure 1

Toulmin Model

Data	Warrant	Claim
Tom Smith		Mr. Smith
1. Played in 25 percent more games	A 25 percent improvement in play deserves	deserves a 25 percent pay increase
2. Hit 25 percent more home runs	A 25 percent increase in pay	
3. Stole 25 percent more bases		
4. Made 25 percent fewer errors		

According to Brockriede and Ehninger (1960), two leading scholars on the Toulmin model, the warrant of a substantive argument may be different types. These types of warrant provide us with different arguments which are useful in conflict resolution. One example is argument from *cause*. In an argument from cause, the warrant takes the data presented and attributes to it a creative or generating power and specifies the nature of the effects that it will produce in the form — the claim. The example in Figure 2 illustrates the point:

Figure 2
Toulmin Model: Causal Warrant

Data	Warrant	Claim
Ballplayer X:	Practice in playing ball will cause an improvement in actual play	Ballplayer X will improve 25 percent this year
1. Practiced batting 25 percent more this spring		
2. Practiced fielding 25 percent more this spring		
3. Reported to training 25% earlier this spring		

The above example of a warrant of cause is just one example of the various types of warrants in argument. While detailed examination of each type of warrant is beyond the scope of this work, arbitration situations often find considerable use of all types of warrants when the various factions present their cases.

The data presented in the argument should conform to the rules of good evidence usually studied in persuasion and debate. This is especially critical to arbitration because the arbitrator is usually skilled in the art of argument and likely to spot weak or insufficient evidence. In court procedures, judges often rule evidence inadmissable for a variety of reasons and skilled labor/management arbitrators can spot specious evidence easily and ignore it in their decisions.

Data may include a variety of types. Examples, illustrations, analogies, testimony, and statistics are typical of the material used as data. When employing examples, one should remember that a sufficient number of representative examples is needed to prove a point. Analogies should include comparisons of items that are similar in all essential ways. Testimony should include statements from objective experts in the area of their expertise. Statistics can be misunderstood or misapplied easily unless the user of the statistic understands what the statistic really represents.

The three essential elements of the Toulmin model—data, warrant, and claim—often are sufficient by themselves to make an argument. However, as arguments become more sophisticated, three secondary elements come into play. They include backing, reservation, and qualifier.

Backing is support for your warrant. At times a warrant requires additional support for the audience to make the mental leap from the data to the claim. This support is called backing.

Reservation is the statement of conditions under which your claim is not true. Perhaps the position you are arguing is true under certain conditions. The reservation allows you to specify the conditions under which it is not true.

Qualifier is the measure of force behind your claim. Qualifiers include statements such as probably, possible, certainly, etc.

These three secondary elements add the following dimensions to the diagram previously presented and are represented in Figure 3.

Figure 3

Toulmin Model: Complete Diagram

Qualifier
1. Mr. Smith might deserve...
2. Mr. Smith probably deserves...

Data	**Warrant**	**Claim**
Tom Smith 1. Played in 25 percent more games. 2. Hit 25 percent more home runs. 3. Stole 25 percent more bases. 4. Made 25 percent fewer errors.	A 25 percent improvement in play deserves a 25 percent increase in pay	Tom Smith deserves a 25 percent pay increase

Backing	**Reservation**
1. Past player settlements have often been based on percentage increases in performance. 2. Mr. Jones improved his performance 25 percent and received a 25 percent increase	1. Mr. Smith was hurt in the last game of the season and it is doubtful whether he can play. 2. The team's attendance was down 50% last year and management may not have any extra money

In an arbitration situation, the complete argument would be presented in this way:

Distinguished Arbitrators: Last year, my client, Mr. Smith, played in 25 percent more games; he hit 25 percent more home runs; he stole 25 percent more bases; his fielding improved 25 percent. I believe that this performance deserves a 25 percent increase in pay for Mr. Smith. Now I think you will remember last year Mr. Jones received a 25 percent increase in pay when his performance improved in a similar way. In addition, every other player on the team received a salary adjustment based on the percentage change in his performance. I can see where this position would be justified if there was some doubt about Smith's health, but he is well. I understand that if the team did not have the money, this might seem too high, but they have sufficient funds. Therefore, I certainly believe you must award Mr. Smith a 25 percent increase in salary.

Of course, both sides would present their best arguments and the arbitrator would decide on the merits of the case.

Sources of Interest

Adler, R.B. *Confidence in communication: a guide to assertive social skills.* New York: Holt, Rinehart and Winston, 1977.

Brockriede, W. and Ehninger, D. Toulmin on argument: an interpretation and application. *Quarterly Journal of Speech,* 1960, 46, 44-53.

Cross, G.P., Names, J.H., and Beck, D. *Conflict and human interaction.* Dubuque, Iowa: Kendall/Hunt, 1979.

Frost, J.H. and Wilmont, W.W. *Interpersonal conflict.* Dubuque, Iowa: W.C. Brown, 1978.

Jandt, F.E. *Conflict resolution through communication.* New York: Harper and Row, 1973.

Keltner, J.W. *Elements of interpersonal communication.* Belmont, California: Wadsworth Publishing, 1973.

Kilmann, R. and Thomas, K. Interpersonal conflict-handling behavior as reflections of jungian personality dimensions. *Psychological Reports,* 1975, 37, 971-980.

Murdock, J. and Semlak, W. "Interpersonal relationships: communication's role in conflict." Illinois Speech and Theatre Association, Peoria, Illinois. November, 1980.

Nye, R.D. *Conflict among humans.* New York: Springer Publishing Company, Inc., 1973.

Rubin, J.Z. and Brown, B.C. *The social psychology of bargaining and negotiation.* New York: Academic Press, 1975.

Schelling, T.C. *The strategy of conflict.* New York: Oxford University Press, 1971.

Semlak, W.D. and Jackson, T.R. *Conflict resolving communication.* In Illinois State University series in Speech Communication, J.F. Cragan (ed.), Dubuque, Iowa: Kendall/Hunt, 1975.

Smith, C.G. (Ed.). *Conflict resolution: contributions of the behavioral sciences.* South Bend, Indiana: Notre Dame University, 1971.

Thomas, K.W. and Pondy, L.R. Toward an "intent" model of conflict management among principle parties. In *Conflict and human interaction* G.R. Cross, H.H. Names and D. Beck (Eds.), Dubuque, Iowa: Kendall/Hunt, 1979.

Toulmin, S. *The uses of argument.* Cambridge, England: Cambridge University Press, 1958.

Villard, K.L. and Whipple, L.J. *Beginnings in relational communication.* New York: John Wiley and Sons, Inc., 1976.

Watzlowick, P.J., Beavin, J., and Jackson, D. *Pragmatics of human communication.* New York: W.W. Norton and Company, 1967.

Notes

Notes